D1007635

INQUIRY AND LEARNING

INQUIRY AND LEARNING

Realizing Science Standards in the Classroom

John W. Layman

with George Ochoa and Henry Heikkinen

College Entrance Examination Board, New York, 1996

John W. Layman is professor of Physics and Science Education, director of the Science Teaching Center, University of Maryland, College Park.

George Ochoa is a principal in Corey & Ochoa, Brooklyn, New York.

Henry Heikkinen is professor of Chemistry, University of Northern Colorado, Greeley.

Robert Orrill is Executive Director of the Office of Academic Affairs, the College Board, New York.

The College Board is a national nonprofit association that champions educational excellence for all students through the ongoing collaboration of nearly 3,000 member schools, colleges, universities, education systems, and associations. The Board promotes—by means of responsive forums, research, programs, and policy development—universal access to high standards of learning, equality of opportunity, and sufficient financial support so that every student is prepared for success in college and work.

Researchers are encouraged to express freely their professional judgment. Therefore, points of view or opinions stated in College Board books do not necessarily represent official College Board position or policy.

Library of Congress Catalog Number: 96-84400

ISBN: 0-87447-547-3

Printed in the United States of America

9 8 7 6 5 4 3 2 1

Contents

Foreword

It is with much pleasure that we make available *Inquiry and Learning: Realizing Science Standards in the Classroom.* This publication completes a series of books on teaching and learning begun earlier in this era of school reform by the College Board's Office of Academic Affairs. Over time, these books have come to be known among educators simply as "the Thinking Series" — a friendly colloquial title that we have now adopted more formally to signify the common theme of these books. Briefly stated, the theme is that the classroom experiences of *all* students, not just a few, should be characterized by frequent opportunities to engage in thoughtful inquiry and learning. Indeed, the larger point is that the entire classroom environment should be oriented toward nurturing what Lauren Resnick and Leo Klopfer have called "a disposition to engage in thinking" (1989). Such a theme, of course, is not new. Earlier in this century, John Dewey repeatedly urged that all of education be organized to support and sustain reflective inquiry. But pursuing this aim has, if anything, become even more difficult for contemporary teachers as the quantity of important information in subject areas has grown at an almost unimaginable rate. Without question, how teachers are to create situations in which students have both time and opportunity to be thoughtful, while they also process and develop needed knowledge, is among the foremost educational challenges of our time.

The books in this series, however, go well beyond a restatement of this long-standing problem. Instead, what they attempt to convey, through both precept and many examples from practice, is how resourceful teachers are succeeding in making their classrooms places in which thinking—not rote behavior—is the rule rather than the exception. In particular, it is especially heartening to see and gain understanding of how this is happening in science classrooms, where the threat of information overload is perhaps most acute. Quite obviously, the enterprise of science is one of the most important shaping influences in the lives of all our citizens, and yet a thoughtful grasp of its workings eludes far too many of us. This is an unacceptable situation in a democracy, and, therefore, science teachers have a vital civic role to play in the nation's future as they work with today's students. This is a charge, we believe, that science educators are now taking up, often imaginatively, and with a great sense of responsibility. Our hope is that this book, which includes the work of some of these teachers, will be useful to all engaged in this important undertaking.

The authors of *Inquiry and Learning* make clear how the intent of this book coincides with, and helps teachers realize, the vision of science education that has emerged recently from the standards-setting efforts of the scientific community. Indeed, each of the books in this series serves well as a practical companion to reform-oriented standards developed for its respective subject area. With more than 60,000 copies already in circulation, the Thinking Series is providing useful insights to teachers across the country regarding how to move from the standards drawing board to classroom action. We believe that *Inquiry and Learning* will add further support for these reform efforts, and, for making this possible, we thank the authors and principal contributors to the book. Very special thanks go also to my colleague, Dorothy Downie, for her steadfast work in bringing the book to completion. Let me also acknowledge the careful editorial attention provided by Hannah Selby. As always, we owe more than can be said to Madelyn Roesch, who has looked after this book with such care from start to finish. All who make books should be fortunate enough to have stalwarts such as these for colleagues.

ROBERT ORRILL
OFFICE OF ACADEMIC AFFAIRS
THE COLLEGE BOARD

Introduction

At a time when science literacy is assuming increasing importance on the national agenda, educators are now able to consult two national documents that provide road maps for improved science learning by all K–12 students—National Science Education Standards (NSES), published by the National Research Council, and Benchmarks for Science Literacy, released by the American Association for the Advancement of Science's Project 2061.

Both reflect strong national consensus on the "desired state" for K–12 science education. They have already influenced policy and practice within most regions of the nation. Nearly all states have or are producing their own statements of what students should know, understand, and be able to do in science. Both Benchmarks and NSES are major influences on that work.

The turbulence, energy, and conflicting priorities swirling around this reform agenda have made it easy to confuse means with ends and to overlook the central, motivating reason for the effort. Fortunately, both NSES and Benchmarks share a common, well-focused, unitary goal—improved science learning by all students. Other components—teaching strategies, assessment, curricula, laboratory activities, professional development, teacher preparation, school resources, policies, public support, and so on—remain important, but serve, in this view, as "means" to the "end" of enhanced student learning.

NSES content standards and Project 2061 Benchmarks independently define the scope, nature, and quality of science learning sought for all students. Many have noted their congruent messages. Indeed, NSES asserts that, "use of the Benchmarks for Science Literacy by state framework committees, school and school-district curriculum committees, and developers of instructional and assessment materials complies fully with the spirit of the content standards" (NSES, p. 15). Similarly, Project 2061's comparison of the two documents concluded: "Given the vast intellectual territory at stake, what is most impressive is the great similarity between the content of two versions, not their differences" (Resources for Science Literacy 1996).

There's also agreement about why enhanced science learning is needed. Richard Klausner, Chairman of the National Committee on Science Education Standards and Assessment, and Bruce Alberts, President of the National Academy of Sciences, express it this way:

> Scientific literacy enables people to use scientific principles and processes in making personal decisions and to participate in discussions of scientific issues that affect society. A sound grounding in science strengthens many of the skills that people use every day, like solving problems creatively, thinking critically, working cooperatively in teams, using technology effectively, and valuing life-long learning. And the economic productivity of our society is tightly linked to the scientific and technological skills of our work force. *(NSES, p. ix)*

In fact, one useful way to think about NSES and Benchmarks is to view them both as operational definitions of the key components of "scientific literacy." Such literacy has been characterized as "the knowledge and habits of mind that people need if they are to live interesting, responsible, and productive lives in a culture in which science, mathematics, and technology are central" (Benchmarks, p. 322).

However, it's not enough merely to identify what all students should know, understand, and be able to do in science— or even to agree about why such learning is important. A central question remains, one that is posed in nearly every standards workshop these days: How does standards-based science instruction look and feel in the classroom?

This book provides a focused, extended response to that question. It does so by considering two related issues: How can teachers cultivate the quality of scientific thinking and understanding defined by standards? And, equally important, how can teachers verify that students have actually attained that level of learning?

True to science itself, the book's answers emerge from gathering, testing, and analyzing data of several types. One important information source tapped by the book is the work and reflection of several real-life, experienced science teachers. Each anchors the book in particular, concrete situations that provide the focus for detailed case studies. Recent research findings and advances in student cognition and learning, which serve as a second "data source" for the book, give a framework for generalizing from those particular classroom practices. Finally, NSES teaching and assessment standards help frame the "content standards in the classroom" story developed in the following pages.

To a large extent, the current reform agenda focuses on ensuring that all K–12 students have the opportunity to experience the best of contemporary science-teaching practice. These "best practices" do not have to be invented; they are already on view in particular classrooms nationwide.

This book highlights some of those productive approaches, viewing them in terms of what's known about student learning and what national consensus clearly affirms are worthy goals for science instruction.

This is a first (or at least very early) contribution to what will likely become a rapidly growing national conversation about the "look and feel" of standards-based science teaching. As such, it is certainly welcomed. May it help stimulate the same quality of thinking and reflection from its readers that it urges for the nation's science students!

HENRY HEIKKINEN

CHAPTER 1

Thinking About Science and Science Teaching

Children and scientists share an outlook on life. "If I do this, what will happen?" is both the motto of the child at play and the defining refrain of the physical scientist. . . . The unfamiliar and the strange—these are the domain of all children and scientists.

(Gleick 1992, 19)

Exploring the World of Science: Bottle Rockets

At the beginning of every school year at Lincoln Southeast High School in Nebraska, Jake Winemiller takes his seniors out to the football field for their first full class in physics. Still not quite reconciled to the end of summer, the students are glad to get out of the classroom and into the warm sunshine, though many have no clue about what they are supposed to do there. The mystery is compounded by the odd apparatus with which Winemiller is working. He pours water into a two-liter pop bottle, label intact, and installs the bottle upside-down in a flat wood-and-metal contraption that sits on the grass and holds the bottle closed with a gasket and pins. Some of the students know what Winemiller is up to from having taken his Physical Science course in the ninth grade; most have heard through the grapevine that this has something to do with rockets, but many find it hard to believe. Connecting a hose from an air compressor, Winemiller forces air into the bottle. He turns to the students and asks them, "What makes a rocket work?"

Some students volunteer ideas—the burning fuel, the pushing of gases against the ground, the kick of a reactive force—none of which are confirmed or denied by Winemiller. He simply says, "Well, keep that question in mind," then asks everyone to stand back, stay low, and watch the bottle. He gives a student the end of a cord that is attached to the apparatus and asks her to give it a good tug when he counts down to one. Then he counts down: "Five . . . four . . . three . . . two . . . one."

The girl pulls the cord. The bottle soars into the Nebraska sky, spurting a long stream of water. It rises higher than any football ever thrown on that field, and then descends, fluttering like a leaf, and finally lands with a thud. The students who remember the experiment from back in the ninth grade smile as if at the sight of an old friend. Others can't believe their eyes. Did a pop bottle just turn into a rocket? Rockets are flaming, steely, billion-dollar things sent on space missions. But this teacher just made a rocket from an old soft-drink container, water, and air.

The field fills with questions:

"How did you do that?"

"How long can you make it stay up there?"

"How high can you make it go?"

Winemiller responds, "Well, I don't know how high it could go. I guess it could go higher."

"Would more water make it go higher?" one student asks.

"What about more air?" asks another.

"How would you find out?" says Winemiller.

Several students in unison say, "We'll have to conduct an experiment," remembering their work in previous science classes. The teacher suggests they work in teams of two to four to design experiments they think will help answer some of their questions.

These physics students have begun to actively explore how a bottle rocket works.

"What exactly are we trying to find out?" Winemiller asks. "What seems like it might get the rocket higher?" one student answers. Winemiller agrees and suggests that the groups get down to the business of specifying some questions.

After a short time, he asks the students in each group to

describe the questions they have come up with and the procedures they propose to use to answer them. As to what influences how high the bottle rocket goes, the students suggest "amount of water," "amount of air," "care with which the cord is pulled," and "whether the launcher is set right on the ground or raised well above the ground."

Each group selects a different experiment and tries to predict in advance what the results of the experiment will be.

The students propose questions as they begin designing their experiments: "It is easy to measure the amount of water, but how do you tell the amount of air?" "Isn't air compressible? If that's the case, is water compressible?" "Will volume be a suitable measure of the amount of air, the amount of water?" "If we stuff more air in, does the volume of air change and what does this do to the water?" The students find that not all these questions can be addressed with the equipment on hand, but the questions are important nonetheless.

Winemiller circulates among the groups as they design their experimental procedures, helping the students refine their language but making sure that they are using terms they understand and not relying on terminology merely for the sake of sounding "scientific." Several groups propose different methods for measuring the height the bottle rocket reached, and they will compare their results after further rocket launches. Of the groups, one employs principles arising from the students' mathematics backgrounds, a second relies on new technology, the third recommends tying a string to the rocket, while the fourth proposes timing the rise and fall, thinking that would be a valid indication of height.

Occasionally Winemiller interrupts the efforts and asks students from different groups to describe particularly interesting questions they have come up with. This inspires a good deal of enthusiasm for the final group reports, which will reveal the answers to many of these questions. The students can draw on their past science experiences, but find that in this practical experiment, with no set procedures to guide them, they have to develop their own ideas and rely on one another for support.

Thanks to this activity, Winemiller has generated excitement and curiosity among his students, which he can build on throughout the course. Winemiller knows that his students will begin to recall the concepts of pressure and volume from their experiences in chemistry, but right now they have the opportunity to apply these ideas in solving the mysteries of the bottle rocket. As they determine how pressure and volume influence how high the bottle rocket goes, each concept will take on deeper meaning. Winemiller also knows that due to its greater compressibility, the volume of air won't be as easy to deal with as the volume of water. From listening to students in previous classes as they carried out their experiments, he knows that he does not have to remind them of the "official science" to be addressed, it will naturally come out of their own efforts. This year he notes that no group has suggested the size of the bottle opening as an option for study, but students in one group said that in chemistry they had dealt with pressure, volume, and temperature ($PV=nRT$), so they elected to vary the temperature of the water in the bottle rocket, not yet recognizing that the T in the gas laws relationship did not apply to the water in the bottle rocket.

Winemiller mused that just a few years ago he would have provided much of the structure and a lot of background information for these activities. But he now recognizes that if he carefully builds on skills students bring to class, such as the ability to suggest experimental designs, to argue about the best way to record and present the data, and to work out explanations that are clear to their classmates, the students themselves will create the structure for these activities and fill in a lot of background information.

Embedding Standards in Classroom Practice

Winemiller is familiar with the national science and mathematics standards and is encouraged by the fact that they reinforce and provide direction for how he and his colleagues are approaching the teaching of science. The national content standards provide clear guidance on the central concepts and procedures that should be learned in science classrooms.

Winemiller knows that the bottle rocket experiment addresses three major goals of teaching science: using scientific principles and procedures appropriately to make decisions; experiencing the richness and excitement of understanding the natural world; and engaging intelligently in public discourse and debate about matters of scientific and technological concern (as students report their experimental observations and conclusions to the rest of the class).

The bottle rocket exercise is part of Winemiller's "framework for year-long and short-term goals for students," representing "content selected to meet the interests, knowledge, understanding, abilities, and experiences of students" (National Science Education Standards, 1996, Teaching Standard A, 30). He is also addressing NSES Teaching Standard B:

Teachers of science guide and facilitate learning. In doing this, teachers:

- focus and support inquiries while interacting with students;

- orchestrate discourse among students about scientific ideas;

- challenge students to accept and share responsibility for their own learning;

- recognize and respond to student diversity and encourage all students to participate fully in science learning;

- encourage and model the skills of scientific inquiry, as well as the curiosity, openness to new ideas and data, and skepticism that characterize science.

(NSES, 1996, Teaching Standard B, 31)

New Pedagogical Constructs

Over the past decade, the groundwork has been laid for new classroom approaches that encourage students to become active learners. All students must employ higher-order thinking skills. Higher-order thinking is defined by Lauren Resnick as nonalgorithmic; complex; amenable to multiple solutions; involving nuanced judgment; employing multiple criteria; uncertain; self-regulating; imposing meaning; and effortful (Resnick 1987, 3). In contrast with previous theory, current views about learning and teaching emphasize "that higher-order skills must suffuse the school program from kindergarten on and in every subject matter" (Resnick 1987, 3). These higher-order thinking skills encourage children to become effective readers and to develop their mathematical skills, both of which are important for learning science.

Winemiller is already familiar with previous work showing that thinking must be the basis of classroom activities for all students in all subjects. Students are to learn and do mathematics, but also to learn to think about mathematics, and about what it means to learn and do mathematics. Winemiller's colleagues who teach language and reading now describe the acquisition of language as learning to communicate and therefore they ground classroom activities in authentic tasks. Winemiller realizes that in their work in small groups, students are strengthening these skills as they struggle to understand the behavior of the bottle rocket. They are generating a set of questions that arise from their personal curiosity and are developing their ideas based on the common experience of seeing a bottle rocket rise into the sky.

The previously dominant view of instruction as direct transfer of knowledge from teacher to student does not fit the current perspective. The present view places the learner's constructive mental activity at the heart of all instructional exchanges. This does not mean that students are left to discover everything for themselves, nor that what they discover and how they choose to describe and account for it are left solely to them. Instruction must provide experiences and information from which learners can build new knowledge. Instruction helps to focus those processes so that the resulting knowledge is both valid and powerful—valid in the sense of describing the world well, or aligning well with the ideas of science, and powerful in the sense of being useful and reliable for these students in many diverse settings.

The Experiments Go On and On

The students are annoyed when the bell rings because they are just getting started. But Winemiller assures them that bottle rocket experimentation will continue tomorrow. "You can't rush science," he tells them. "We're not going to stop until we get some answers."

The class soon finds that questions continue. The bottle rocket exploration does not end the next day, or the next week, or the week after that. It goes on at various times for nearly two months as students explore which air pressure works best at each volume, whether the rocket needs water at all to fly, and whether smaller or larger bottles improve performance. Student groups investigate how fast the rocket is going, how far it flies after the fuel is spent, and how long they can keep it flying.

These explorations require an intellectual framework—concepts that help make sense of what is happening. As new concepts are needed, Winemiller helps students understand such things as velocity, acceleration, mass, force, thrust, gravity, friction, air resistance, conservation of energy, density, pressure, and fluid dynamics. He leads them to reflect on the conceptual implications of what they have observed. And he tells stories of Tsiolkovsky and Goddard and von Braun and how they grappled with similar theoretical and technological problems. Something of the richness of rocket history comes out—the development of rockets as bomb-carrying weapons in World War II and their later adaptation as vehicles for exploring space.

The students are continually encouraged to translate new experiences and concepts into workable solutions through experimentation. Through leaps of insight, trial and error, argument, and frustration, students apply the concepts of physics to expand what they know and are able to do.

Just Another Approach, or More?

What exactly does Winemiller accomplish by launching bottle

rockets with his physics students? What are science teachers like him—in biology, chemistry, earth science—doing when they de-emphasize lecture and "cookbook lab" approaches in favor of teaching science through hands-on, "minds-on," process-oriented, inquiry-based investigations? Is it merely a matter of coaxing students to learn content that would otherwise bore them? Or are their students learning something that can't be taught any other way?

An investigative or inquiry-based approach such as Winemiller's can indeed help students learn the important concepts, processes, and habits of mind of science, and also something more. The students experience firsthand what science is—an ongoing, complex enterprise of the mind, conducted collaboratively with practical consequences for human welfare. They learn this by doing what scientists do—applying intellectual processes to the task of producing and testing knowledge about the natural world. Students are not only introduced to the body of ideas called scientific knowledge, but also themselves become thinkers about the unknown and builders of knowledge. ■

CHAPTER 2

Doing Science

Knowledge cannot spring from experience alone, but only from comparison of the inventions of mind with observed fact.

(Albert Einstein)

Science as Inquiry

The National Science Education Standards identify Science as Inquiry as a central learning goal for all students. The intended meaning of this important content standard is clarified in this way:

> The standard should not be interpreted as adovcating a "scientific method." The conceptual and procedural abilities suggest a logical progression, but they do not imply a rigid approach to scientific inquiry. On the contrary, they imply co-development of the skills of students acquiring science knowledge, in using high-level reasoning, in applying their existing understanding of scientific ideas, and in communicating scientific information. This standard cannot be met by having the students memorize the abilities and understandings. It can be met only when students frequently engage in active inquiries.
>
> *(NSES 1996, 144–145)*

There are, however, features common to what *Science for All Americans* refers to as the Scientific World View that, to some extent, distinguish science from other modes of knowing:

■ The world is understandable.

■ Scientific ideas are subject to revision.

■ Scientific knowledge is durable.

■ Science cannot provide complete answers to all questions.

- Science is inquiry.
- Science demands evidence.
- Science is a blend of logic and imagination.
- Science explains and predicts.
- Scientists try to identify and avoid bias.
- Science is not authoritarian.
- Science is a complex social activity.
- There are generally accepted ethical principles in the conduct of science.
- Scientists participate in public affairs both as specialists and as citizens.

(Science for All Americans)

Ideally, students should emerge from the science classroom with an appreciation of the fact that science is at once a body of knowledge and a dynamic questing activity.

When students pursue inquiry-based activities, they learn about many of the features listed above through experience. Both teachers and students, however, must understand the significance of these characteristics and recognize that they are valid in both the research laboratory and in the science classroom. If students are familiar with the scientific worldview, they do not need a particularly worded or sequenced statement of a "scientific method." In physicist Percy Bridgman's words, "The scientific method, as far as it is a method, is nothing more than doing one's damnedest with one's mind, no holds barred" (Bridgman 1960).

If students are to understand what it means in science to do "one's damnedest with one's mind," and if, as urged in the National Science Education Standards and in Benchmarks for Science Literacy, this goal applies to all students, new questions need to be asked. What aspects of doing science are discernible at every stage in a scientific investigation, whether it is being conducted by students in their classrooms or scientists in their laboratories? How can the identification of these aspects lead to the development of a scientifically literate person?

Exploring the World of Science: Slime Mold

Peggy O'Neill Skinner, a biology teacher in Seattle, Washington, introduces her students to observation and experiment in their study of slime mold. Usually working in groups of two or three, her students first learn how to grow slime mold on a petri dish in a 2 percent agar solution with oatmeal as food. In the process of learning to grow the mold, students begin making general observations. Skinner then asks her students to come up with some questions about slime mold that can be answered within a day by making observations of the slime mold on the dish. Typical initial questions include "Why is it yellow?" and "What kind of living thing is it?" Through discussion, Skinner helps her students see that these questions cannot be answered in the specified time span with the materials at hand. She reminds them, "You've got to find your answer by observing what happens on this dish today or overnight."

The groups of students then return to the task of determining what they can observe in a short time. What do slime molds do every day? They eat and they grow. One student asks, "How do they eat?" This sounds like a good question until a classmate wonders how they will answer it and the group realizes that the question is too broad to resolve in one day. Something more specific is needed. "Can anything block a slime mold from getting its food?" This is not specific enough, either. How can you test "anything," Skinner points out, when framing a question that can be answered experimentally means focusing on a few specific factors or variables. A student playing with the corner of a page of her notebook makes a connection and asks, "What about paper? Could paper block a slime mold from eating?"

Now they're on to something. A paper barrier is a variable that can be tested. The students begin designing an experiment to test the idea. This leads to other questions. One student imagines a water barrier, like a castle moat. "Can a slime mold cross water to get its food?" "What if you put table salt in the water?" someone else asks. "Salt might kill it—might dry it up. It wouldn't want to cross salt."

In another group, a student thinks about the cover of the agar dish. "What if you put the food on the inside top cover of the dish? Can a slime mold crawl upside down to get it?" Another student asks if the slime mold "knows" where the food is and "knows" to climb there. "Can it act against the downward pull of gravity and climb up the side of the dish? Can it hang upside down on the cover of the dish and progress across this surface?"

Each group of students works on a narrow question, but they share what they have learned in a slime mold seminar. This provides everybody with the opportunity to compare what they have seen and learned and broaden their understanding by thinking about questions and experiments that they themselves did not consider.

As with the questions arising from the bottle rocket experiment, the questions Skinner's students ask draw on their prior knowledge as well as their own curiosity about slime mold. Students' visions of slime mold going up the walls of the dish do not imply that slime mold can somehow "resist gravity." These students are probably drawing on an unscientific notion that a bird or someone in a circus act is somehow exempt from the gravitational force that affects the rest of us. A student's pleasure in seeing things that seem to resist gravity likely drives the question. Similarly, the insight that salt may be a danger to a slime mold may come from having heard that slugs are killed that way and from an interest in seeing it happen. The questions do not come directly from observing the agar dish, but from the interaction of students' beliefs, experiences, and motivations with sensory information, the observed behavior of the slime mold on the dish, and social constraints, in this case, the teacher's deadline and specifications for how their initial research is to be done.

Learning and the Scientific Approach

Can the characteristics of a scientist outlined at the beginning of this chapter be identified in the activities of students pursuing an experiment such as the one on slime mold? Let's look at them one by one and relate them to what we're examining in this book.

- **The world is understandable.** Students begin their study of slime mold and its behavior using their own terms and collaborating with one another in their efforts. They learn to respect differing points of view and may consult formal resources as well. They find that their understanding has grown considerably as a result of participating in these investigations.

- **Scientific ideas are subject to revision.** Some of the ideas students initially offer to support their observations don't withstand careful scrutiny through experiment.

- **Scientific knowledge is durable.** Some of the students who pursue historical accounts of slime mold behavior find early observations that still hold true today, while other findings have to be reconsidered.

- **Science cannot provide complete answers to all questions.** Students find themselves asking questions that imply volition on the part of slime mold. They learn that they cannot determine volition from the experiments and observations they are conducting.

- **Science is inquiry.** Students come to recognize that each of them has an inquiring mind. They don't all start with the same background, nor will they all pursue the same path, but they all participate in inquiry and contribute to the group's shared pursuit of understanding the characteristics of slime mold.

- **Science demands evidence.** As students begin to get answers to some of the questions raised by the various groups, they learn that the answers must be accompanied by evidence obtained through observations and experiments, and from other sources of information. This is how scientific ideas undergo revision.

- **Science is a blend of logic and imagination.** Some of the most interesting questions arise from students' imaginations. Conjecture about the nature and behavior of slime mold is encouraged, but students learn that conjecture should lead to designing an experiment or consulting other sources of information that confirm their speculations.

- **Science explains and predicts.** As students raise their initial questions, they realize that these are often predictions of the behavior of slime mold that can only be confirmed or rejected by observation. When the observations are made and explanations offered, students find there are even more questions to ask and try to answer.

- **Scientists try to identify and avoid bias.** Some of the students feel uneasy with the term "slime" mold, which conjures up visions from horror tales and movies. It takes time for them to understand that this living organism interacts and participates in the natural world and takes its rightful place among biological organisms that do not have the "slimy" connotation.

- **Science is not authoritarian.** Students discover that slime mold is not simply a static and fully understood topic of inquiry presented in a textbook. Some of the questions that students ask about slime mold aren't answered in their textbook and remain for investigation.

- **Science is a complex social activity.** Students learn, with Skinner's help, that the questions each group elects to study are the result of negotiation. Some students can't persuade the group to choose their question, even though another group might focus on something similar.

- **There are generally accepted ethical principles in the conduct of science.** Some students are disappointed that their predictions prove to be wrong. Some accuse others of fudging their data to obtain better results. Some realize that their experimental design is faulty, thus preventing them from making the observations that they had hoped to make. All these experiences lead to interesting discussions of the general principles and ethics of conducting science.

■ ***Scientists participate in public affairs both as specialists and as citizens.*** Within Skinner's class are students who will go on to major in science or mathematics, as well as others with interests in the arts or literature. Students respond from differing frames of reference and bring different sets of skills and interests to the classroom, but they learn to value all contributions from within their learning community. Students may use their talents, perhaps in art or photography, to supplement or illustrate their work.

Slime Mold and More

The slime mold activities obviously did not constitute the whole year's work in biology. Skinner introduced a wide variety of activities, but students found that the early slime mold work sensitized them to ask broad, inquiry-based questions whatever the focus of study. They also realized that they were asking questions that even Skinner couldn't answer, proof that they were learning to "do science."

During the slime mold inquiry, Skinner was also engaged in something that the national standards have identified as central—conducting an ongoing assessment. She collected information about students' understanding and adjusted her teaching approach on the basis of the information she gathered. In the next chapter, we'll examine this issue in greater depth—the challenge of cultivating students' understanding of science. ■

Below is a sample report from one group in Skinner's class, along with her comments.

next
question

Experiment #2 - Can physarum grow up a wall and then upside down? (Can it resist gravity?) Materials : 98 grams of water, 2 grams of agar, one petri dish, sterile tweezers, physarum, oatmeal, microscope. Procedure : Make a double batch of the agar solution as shown above and pour half of it into the bottom of the petri dish, then fill the top of the petri dish two thirds full and allow it to dry while being tilted at a slight angle. After they have hardened, place a piece of the physarum, (while in it's sclerotium stage), with sterile tweezers onto the bottom of the petri dish. Next stick a piece of yeast *oatmeal?* into the top of the petri dish so that it is sticking half in and half out. Add a drop of water to the bottom of the petri dish for moisture, and place the lid onto the petri dish. The agar on the top of the petri dish should have dried in a way so that both sections of agar touch at some point. The yeast and physarum should be close by. Place in a dark room overnight.

Results and Conclusion : After doing this experiment I found that the physarum is able to climb up an agar wall and then grow along an agar ceiling in search of food. After I took the lid off, I looked at the physarum that had grown onto the ceiling and found it to be alive and healthy. Gravity seems to have no effect on the slime mold. *great question for & research* *an answer*

how did you get to this question?

Experiment #3 - Can physarum grow across water? Materials - Agar, physarum, exacto knife, sterile tweezers, petri dish, salt and water. Procedure : Follow the procedure at the beginning of this lab. After you have let it grow overnight, cut a hole into the agar, (about one third the size of the total agar). Make sure you still have most of the physarum on the petri dish. Fill the hole with a solution of 3% salt water. *why?* Scrape off the physarum from the piece of agar you have cut and then cut a small circle about the size of a dime from it. Place this piece in the center of the lake you have made in your petri dish. On top of your new island place a piece of yeast. Put the lid on the petri dish and place it in a dark room overnight. *oatmeal?*

Results and Conclusion : From doing this experiment I found that physarum can't cross salt water. (At-least not 3% salt water). There were no visible signs of it having or attempting to cross the water.

Discussion and Conclusion : By performing experiments on the slime mold *physarum* our class learned many different things. Courtney and Dierdra answered the question : Can physarum cross a moist barrier to find food? By making an agar mountain in the middle of their petri dish and placing physarum on one side and food on the other, they found the physarum crossed the dish in a circle and found the food. When they put the yeast closer to the ˙physarum in their next test, they found it went straight to it. This proved that physarum can somehow detect food and head straight for it. Sarah, Ali, Jennie G., and Joey found in a simular experiment that physarum is unable to cross a dry surface, (paper). By creating a paper barrier between the physarum and the food, the physarum was unable to reach the food.

Sarah's group also did an experiment to answer the question : What is the physarum's reaction to salt? They found that it didn't like to go near it. If it had gone near it, they would probably have found that it would have osmosisized itself to death.

Fred found interesting results with a experiment of his own on the reaction of physarum to oil. His results showed that it ate it, and then digested it. After doing so, he noted that it created antibodies? and fruiting bodies called badhimia.?

The group consisting of Jacob, Sarah and Malery also preformed a successful experiment in which they found the physarum gives off acid when digesting its food. By mixing a Congo red indicator into their agar and then noticing its color change from red to blue after eating oatmeal, they proved that it does in fact digest its food with acid. This group also found that scraping and cutting the slime mold has no effect on the structure as a whole.

Adam and C.J. were the last group in our class to perform experiments on physarum. By isolating certain sections of the slime mold, they discovered that even though it was amputated, it still continued to grow. After performing these experiments on the physarum and sharing them with the rest of the class, our knowledge of what had once been an unknown object to us had grown greatly.

did you do this also?

CHAPTER 3

Understanding Science

I do not know what I may appear to the world, but to myself I seem to have been only like a boy playing on the seashore and diverting myself in now and then finding a smooth pebble or a prettier shell than ordinary, while the great ocean of truth lay all undiscovered before me.

(Sir Isaac Newton)

We now turn to the theme "science for all." If we are designing instructional programs for students and teachers that honor the "science for all" concept, we must ensure "understanding for all" as well. In this chapter we'll examine what students know, should understand, and be able to do. Understanding from the teacher's perspective will be addressed in Chapter 4, Teaching Science.

Exploring the World of Science: Maplecopters

Toys are a good way to introduce the concept of models, which are central to understanding science. In the activity "Exploring the Maplecopter" from the Connecticut Common Core of Learning Assessment Project (Baron 1993), the motion of a falling maple seed is investigated using a paper helicopter as a simplified, controllable model of the natural object. Modeling scientific concepts with toys can be fun, but it is also an excellent teaching strategy for fostering scientific thinking.

While carrying out their investigations, students such as those quoted below encountered technical problems constructing a paper helicopter that will model the motion of a falling maple seed.

Steve (as Richard stands on a stool and drops the paper helicopter straight down): It's not spinning. Why isn't it spinning?

The students try making helicopters of different sizes with different wing lengths and with different numbers of paper clips to add weight at the bottom. Their early frustration is exceeded only by their jubilation when they are finally successful:

Steve (as he drops a paper helicopter that has just the right spinning motion): Yes!

Richard: Did you see that one?

Barbara: You took off more weight?

Richard: Yes.

Barbara: So we know that's what makes it go down, it's the weight at the tip—the more weight at the tip . . .

(The trial is repeated with a large and a small helicopter; the students stop, smile, laugh.)

Barbara: It works! It works! It works!

Richard: Look, I got this one up too.

Barbara: So we got a big one and a little one to work.

Despite technical success, doubts about the appropriateness of using a paper helicopter to model the motion of a maple seed begin to emerge. Richard questions whether varying the length of the wings on the paper helicopter will really allow them to figure out the effect of air resistance on a maple seed:

Richard: I don't see any parallelism.

Barbara: There's a lot of parallelism.

Richard: This thing (*the maple seed*) has two things to hold it. This thing (*the paper helicopter*) only has one thing to hold it.

Barbara: We could scrap it. It's up to you.

Richard: I'm just saying we should think about it.

Barbara: It took me two hours to make them, but I'm willing to scrap them. If you think this has nothing to do with the wing here, we can scrap it.

Richard's question forces the other students to reevaluate this particular model. It also shows them that experimental design is not a matter of simple, direct observations of nature, but the creative framing of those observations in theoretical context. Therefore, even in planning their experiment, the students have to consider how they will interpret the significance of their data and whether their interpretations will be valid. Despite her displeasure, Barbara perceives correctly that if the team itself is not convinced of the validity of its assumptions, a new experimental model must be designed.

If experimental planning has been solid, conducting the actual experiment may go like clockwork. As a teacher describes the maplecopter experiment, "When students finally begin recording data, the work becomes almost prosaic." At one stage, for example, a bar is set up to indicate a constant height; from that height, one student drops a paper helicopter with one paper clip attached to the tip. "One paper clip," he announces. Another student times the fall with a stopwatch; another records the measurements. Another paper clip is added. "Two paper clips," the student announces; again the fall is timed, again the data are recorded.

Inquiry-Based Learning

Understanding for all means focusing on inquiry as the mode of learning in a teaching setting in which students are actively involved and aware of the special character of science. The inquiry mode is an empirically verifiable, productive way to cultivate understanding, and is a central theme in both the NSES and AAAS Benchmarks documents.

Science teachers in classrooms where the inquiry mode takes center stage create situations that catch the attention of students and raise questions that draw them into the world of scientific investigation. This initial stage setting provides the motivation needed for the challenge of doing science. Later in the process, other aspects of the inquiry mode reinforce the student's motivation—teamwork, competition, making sense out of what seems mystifying, successfully defending findings before an audience of critics. The first step, however, is to capture the students' attention and arouse their interest.

Once drawn into inquiry-based learning by launching bottle

rockets, studying slime mold, dropping maplecopters, or participating in other experimental projects, students engage in a wide range of activities. Teachers then face the challenge of assessing their students' knowledge, understanding, and ability to do.

Assessment and Learning: Two Sides of the Same Coin

In an inquiry-based classroom, it is frequently difficult to separate assessment activities from ongoing teaching and learning. Assessment and learning are viewed as two sides of the same coin. One goal in these classrooms is to develop within the students the ability to monitor their own progress and that of the class as a whole. To facilitate this, teachers can share with individual students and groups guidelines that describe the criteria that will be used to evaluate their demonstrated performance. Using these, students can learn to monitor their own progress as they carry out their tasks or projects and to experiment with different approaches to problem solving.

A variety of scoring rubrics have been developed to evaluate the performance of groups and individual students. This sample provides a set of categories for evaluation, each with two subcategories and associated scores shown in parentheses:

Demonstrated competence
Exemplary response (6),
Competent response (5),

Satisfactory response
With minor flaws but satisfactory (4),
Serious flaws but nearly satisfactory (3),

Inadequate response
Begins, but fails to complete problem (2),
Unable to begin effectively (1).

(CAP Generalized Rubric in Herman, Ashbacher, and Winters 1992, 56)

In the full document, each subcategory is documented with explanations of what to look for in students' performances, how to distinguish performances, and how to do the evaluations. Theoretically, all students could achieve 6s and would not have the perception that their success was at the expense of someone else's, but rather that their mutual support of one another ensured the success of the entire learning community.

If the same or similar rubrics are used in all science and math classes and in a variety of other subject areas and grade levels, students will become very familiar with them and will enter each new course knowing how their performance will be evaluated.

Thinking Is Basic

If thinking is the basis of all learning, then we must sharpen our understanding of just what thinking is and what it entails. Jim Greeno (1992), considering both science and mathematics, discusses thinking and makes a special point of distinguishing between "thinking with the basics" and "thinking is basic." He describes these two perspectives in terms of classroom differences.

In thinking with the basics, classroom teaching provides fundamental scientific and mathematical information that students can use to think scientifically or mathematically after they have mastered a significant body of knowledge, and if they are sufficiently talented and motivated (Greeno 1992, 39).

From the thinking with the basics perspective, the fact that students seldom think scientifically reflects a shortcoming in the students. They don't have the necessary talent or motivation or they haven't been trained adequately in the general skill of thinking. Thinking with the basics presupposes a sharp distinction between knowledge and thinking. A great deal of knowledge can be acquired without much thought, but you can't do much thinking without knowledge! Thinking is like manufacturing, with knowledge supplying the new materials and energy, while ideas, understanding, solutions to problems, and the like are the output. A good stock of materials of a refined sort is needed to produce the finished product.

On the other hand, "thinking is basic" is a very different view of classroom teaching. Here, learning to think scientifically and mathematically is a major focus of classroom activity from the very first day of the course. Thinking is a natural human activity, and students' failure to learn to think scientifically is not their fault but reflects characteristics of the classroom setting that do not support thinking as the principal activity (Greeno 1992, 39).

The ability to think is natural to humans, but it is a trait that must be developed. And there is plenty of room for variation in talent or acquired ability. If we approach the ability to think as a natural human activity, then its development depends mainly on providing opportunities to think and continually challenging what we believe we already know. The ability to think is developed through participation in a series of increasingly more challenging activities. From the outset, they involve thinking rather than withholding the opportunity to think until sufficient "materials"—information and knowledge—have been acquired.

From this perspective, thinking is the main focus of all learning activities, enabling students to develop their ability to think through elaboration, refinement, and modification of the abilities they bring to the classroom (Greeno 1992, 40).

The thinking is basic view implies that the very thought processes students already use (sometimes unwittingly) to understand history or foreign languages are the same processes they must use to think scientifically.

Lauren Resnick identified three interrelated aspects of learning that together call for instructional theories very different from those that grew out of earlier psychologies:

- Learning is a process of knowledge construction, not of knowledge recording or absorption.

- Learning is knowledge-dependent; people use current knowledge to construct new knowledge.

- Learning is highly tuned to the situation in which it takes place.   *(Resnick 1989, 1)*

Resnick also suggested that instruction must stimulate active knowledge-constructing processes among individuals who may initially doubt their own ability for or right to engage in independent thinking (Resnick 1989, 2). This perspective certainly complements our commitment to teach all students to think scientifically.

"The most important single message of modern research on the nature of thinking is that the kinds of activities traditionally associated with thinking are not limited to advanced levels of development. Instead, these activities are an intimate part of even elementary levels of reading, mathematics, and other branches of learning—when learning is proceeding well." (Resnick 1978, 8). This means that the kinds of activities pursued in all classrooms, not just in science classrooms, must be accessible to all students, that each student must be actively involved in thinking, and that the ability to think is not something limited to students who enter the classroom with a full stock of basic information.

The Ability to "Do" Science

Having established an ability to think, just what are students who understand science expected to be able to do, and why is this an important element of thinking?

A variety of skills associated with the process of scientific inquiry are germane to being able to do, including:

- describing objects and events
- asking questions
- constructing explanations
- testing explanations against current scientific knowledge
- communicating ideas to others.

(National Science Education Standards 1996, 2)

These skills will be acquired only if students have ample opportunity to practice them and reflect on the processes by which they are acquired. Fortunately, these skills can be developed by studying any science subject if the classroom is inquiry-based and honors thinking as the primary activity. Let's look at one example from physics and a second from biology with a bit of chemistry.

Exploring the World of Science: Putting Socks on Thermometers

Inspired by a suggestion from Ronald Sass, a biology professor at Rice University, Earl Carlyon, who teaches physics in Manchester, Connecticut, asks his twelfth-grade students the following question: "What would happen if you took three identical thermometers, all reading the same temperature, and wrapped them in three different socks—one wool, one silk, and one cotton—then left them in the classroom for 24 hours? What temperature would each thermometer read and why?"

Unknown to the students, Carlyon is conducting an experiment to test a hypothesis of his own. Sass had reported that a group of 25 college graduates had given the wrong answer to this question, erroneously responding that the thermometer in the wool sock would reach a higher temperature than the others. Sass concluded that this pointed to a widespread misconception about heat sources, even among individuals with college educations. Carlyon thought the claim was farfetched: "I didn't really think people were that naive." As it turned out, he, too, was proved wrong.

In groups of three, Carlyon's students struggle to formulate their hypotheses. None of the groups correctly predict that all thermometers will read the same, but all groups show a combination of creativity and logical reasoning in reaching their erroneous predictions. Most draw an implicit, mistaken analogy between thermometers and warm-blooded creatures like themselves, imagining what they would feel like wearing wool or cotton or silk.

"Wool," says one student. "I go camping wearing wool, and you jump in the water, you're still warm. Silk doesn't keep you warm."

Starting from this mistaken assumption, one group of students makes elaborate predictions about what the temperature change will be for each fabric. The wool-covered thermometer will rise about 10 degrees, the cotton-covered one will stay at the same temperature plus or minus 2 degrees, and the silk-covered one will drop 10 degrees.

One girl in another group is heading for the right answer, but is talked out of it by her classmates. She questions the prevailing wisdom that the wool-covered thermometer will be the warmest.

Amy: Where would the heat come from?

Bill: Inside!

Roberta: Inside! You know, how you close up—(demonstrating with her collar)—like when you zip up.

Amy: I know, but it doesn't have life or anything.

Roberta: I don't care.

Bill: It won't be affected by that.

Amy continues to express doubts about her classmates' claims, and finally Roberta presses Amy for her reasoning.

Roberta (to Amy): Well, what do you think?

Amy: I think they're gonna be all the same.

Roberta (looking skeptical): You think all of them?

Bill: But when you wear wool, it's always warm.

Roberta: It's always warm.

Amy: But we have a body temperature, that's why it goes up. This doesn't have a body temperature, it's just a stick.

The group is at an impasse. They finally settle the debate, as Carlyon puts it, by "social contract." They agree that many factors, too many to be calculated in advance, might affect the outcome.

Roberta: Maybe it depends on how it is outside, I don't know. It all depends.

Amy: It depends on the time, the temperature, and the wind, the mile-per-hour and stuff.

Roberta: They should all stay the same temperature. But it all depends though. It still depends.

Rather than settling on a clear prediction, this group of students muddy their hypothesis, saying essentially that no consistent results can be expected. In deciding this, they dismiss Amy's suggestions.

At this point, Carlyon's students carry out the experiment and discover that the temperature of each thermometer remains the same regardless of which material is wrapped around it. This result can now be compared with their predictions and hypotheses. Perhaps they will recognize that some of the hypotheses offered before conducting the experiment were as much socially as scientifically derived, and realize that Amy's suggestions were correct after all. Thinking is the fundamental activity that occurs throughout the whole process, with the experimentally derived results influencing the final outcome of this whole thinking activity.

Why Cut Potatoes Turn Brown

Peggy Skinner challenges her biology students to isolate the factors that cause a cut potato to turn brown. In class discussion, she makes clear that "air" is too vague an answer: if air is involved, what in air is the significant factor (or factors)? The students soon realize that to answer this question would require not one, but a series of experiments. In deciding how to isolate and test the effects of the various components of air, the students have to draw on previous exercises, applying their knowledge creatively in a new context. They generated oxygen using liver and hydrogen peroxide; they decreased the amount of oxygen within a bell jar by burning a candle; and they generated carbon dioxide with Alka-Seltzer for experiments where carbon dioxide was used to anesthetize fruit flies. The knowledge students gained from these previous activities must be assembled in a new protocol; variables must be manipulated one at a time, while controlling for other variables. To complicate matters, the students realize that the gases in air are not the only variables; something in the potato must be interacting with air to cause the potato to turn brown. That process, too, will have to be isolated.

Students' understanding of experimental procedures and findings is often assessed through individual and group oral and written reports. When students pursue different lines of inquiry about a single topic, presenting and sharing results gives them an opportunity to build on each other's research. After several groups of Skinner's students have independently researched slime mold, they listen to each other's oral presentations before writing their final reports. "Then," says Skinner, "they can say, 'Well, from Jenny we know that a slime mold can cross a moist barrier, but I had a dry barrier and it didn't cross that, so maybe it's the dryness that blocks it.'" If two similar experiments result in contradictory findings, the groups may decide to rerun the experiments, thus illustrating the importance of replicability of results in science.

Here is the written report of one student in Skinner's biology class:

Using the information from my experiment and others, I have come to the conclusion that the browning of potatoes once they have been exposed is caused by a chemical reaction between something in the potato and something else in air. I reached this conclusion by looking mainly at two things, the fact that if a potato is submerged in water or oil and is cut off from contact with air then it will not turn brown and that the browning process is slowed if the potato is placed in a cool place (as shown by Kevin).

From past lab experience, I know that a chemical reaction can be slowed by dropping the temperature in which the reaction takes place. Once I figured this out I tried to figure out what it is in the potato and air that cause the reaction. As for the potato, I did not do any tests such as testing the starch content. Perhaps I believe that it is sugar just because I know that apples also turn brown when exposed and that apples have sugar but this is only a guess. I do however believe that I know what it is in air that causes the reaction: OXYGEN. I have two facts to support this. The first is the test that Steve Fuhs ran on his potato slice. He placed a slice of potato in a jar turned over on a table with a lit candle. The candle used up all the oxygen in the jar and then burnt out. The potato slice did not turn brown in the oxygen free enviornment. The other reason why I believe that browning is caused by oxygen is that many other things, such as metals, can be changed by oxidation. If oxygen or sugar, as I believe, are taken away then the potato will not turn brown.

Carlyon's physics students were in the same position as the student who wrote the cut potato report when they put their hypothesis about the sock-covered thermometers to the test. After being left in the classroom for 24 hours, the wool-covered, cotton-covered, and silk-covered thermometers all read the same temperature. (Students guessed that the small temperature variations that were observed were due to slight differences in the thermometers. Determining what constitutes significant data is another important aspect of drawing conclusions.) The students' predictions that the wool-covered thermometer would read the highest, the silk-covered one the lowest, and the cotton-covered one in the middle were apparently refuted. Were the results due to a flaw in the experimental design? Should more care have been taken to use fabrics of equal thickness? Would different weather conditions cause the thermometers to read in the predicted way?

Far from being unscientific in not immediately rejecting their hypothesis, Carlyon's students were exercising appropriate caution about drawing far-reaching conclusions from a single experiment. They were using critical and logical thinking. They could not readily abandon their present hypothesis without replacing it with some other explanation, and they could not construct a new explanation with the knowledge they had at hand.

It might be tempting to infer that employing inquiry-based science is only appropriate for advanced students. However, as Skinner states:

> The reason that I adopted a collaborative approach to learning about my "model organisms" is that I felt that it met the needs of a broader range of students. If all students do the same exercises, more able students often just do them faster, less able ones do them more slowly or perhaps do not even finish them. An approach that gives each student or perhaps small groups of students the freedom to explore something that they are curious about allows them to proceed at their own pace. Also, when they get to the point of sharing their information and process with the rest of the class, everybody learns even if the exercise is very simple. Last year when my 9–10s were doing this [the

slime mold experiment], one student who had had extreme difficulty the first semester of biology was interested in the healing that took place when the slime mold was cut. He sliced and diced some of the slime mold and ended up putting some of the pieces near each other. They rejoined into one larger piece. This was a very simple experiment, but it stimulated some of the most interesting conversation when he presented his ideas to the class. If the information is new, even the smallest piece clarifies everyone's big picture. The key is to have students doing different things with the same organism. Incidentally, this student kept his slime mold alive long after the class work ended, thus sustaining his interest in biology to the point of exiting the second semester with an improved grade.

While activities take more organization and equipment in a larger class, the experiment's parameters . . . time limits, simple materials . . . still permit them to be done. Every time a teacher lets students go in different directions, it is chaotic at best, but from that chaos emerges science at its best! Curiosity, questions, sharing ideas, seeing patterns . . . couldn't be better.

The four activities highlighted in this chapter, maplecopters, thermometers and coverings, observations of slime molds, and the browning potatoes, should involve all students, and result in each student gaining knowledge, understanding, and the ability to do.

How to make the transition to a more inquiry-based science program is explored in the next chapter. ■

CHAPTER 4

Teaching Science

*Schools should pick the most important concepts and skills to empha-
size so that they can concentrate on the quality of understanding rather
than on the quantity of information presented.*

(Rutherford and Ahlgren 1987)

T he preceding chapter illustrated the potential of inquiry-
centered activities to foster students' growth as scientific thinkers. What central elements need to be addressed
in adopting or changing to a more investigative or inquiring approach? What has to happen in a science classroom
for meaningful learning to take place?

The National Science Education Standards describe what
teachers of science at all grade levels should know and be able
to do. These are divided into six areas:

1. The planning of inquiry-based science programs.

2. The actions taken to guide and facilitate student learning.

3. The assessments made of teaching and student learning.

4. The development of environments that enable students to
   learn science.

5. The creation of communities of science learners.

6. The planning and development of the school science
   program.

(NSES 1996, 4)

Adopting a Different Instructional Approach

If a teacher's approach to science instruction does not already
focus on inquiry-based investigations and experiments, what
can he or she do to change? Does it require a complete over-

haul or are there gradual ways to get started? What is the optimum balance between student-driven investigations and teacher direction?

Ronald Bonnstetter, director of Secondary Science Education at the University of Nebraska, Lincoln, suggests that change has to occur incrementally. "You take one day's lesson or one or two days—you've got to start at that level. You start by asking a real question, a question each student can answer. "What's the pH of the soil in your backyard?" When the teacher has gained more experience and confidence using an inquiry-based approach, a whole unit might be centered on an array of questions or activities; later, every unit in the course can include some component of this approach.

None of the teachers who contributed to the making of this book employs an inquiry-based approach as the sole pedagogical technique. All balance student-directed inquiry with other classroom activities—class discussion, reading, solving written problems, elementary activities to introduce skills, films, tapes, and transparencies. The exact balance varies from teacher to teacher, as does the preferred method for combining different teaching strategies.

Inquiry-Centered Instruction

Inquiry-centered instruction may be described in terms of a set of characteristics shared by teachers adopting this approach. Such teachers:

- encourage and accept student autonomy and initiative;
- use raw data and primary sources, along with manipulative, interactive, and physical materials;
- when framing tasks, use cognitive terminology such as classify, analyze, predict, and create;
- allow student responses to drive lessons, shift instructional strategies, and alter content;
- familiarize themselves with students' understandings of concepts before sharing their own understandings of those concepts;

- encourage students to engage in dialogue, both with the teacher and with one another;
- encourage student inquiry by posing thoughtful, open-ended questions and asking students to question each other;
- seek elaboration of students' initial responses;
- engage students in experiences that pose contradictions to their initial hypotheses and then encourage discussion;
- allow time after posing questions;
- provide time for students to construct relationships and create metaphors; and
- nurture students' natural curiosity.

(Brooks and Brooks 1993, 102–18)

The characteristics of inquiry-based teachers listed above apply to all classrooms, not just those teaching science. This description also reinforces the point of view of the NSES Teaching Standards.

The Learning-Cycle Approach to Instruction

The learning cycle is a multiple-stage research-based approach to science instruction that outlines an effective way of encouraging students to build a useful knowledge base through increased understanding. Its original three-stage form (Atkin and Karplus 1962) can be summarized as follows: In Stage 1, students are provided with an open-ended opportunity to interact with carefully chosen sets of materials (physical or written). As was done in the slime mold experiment, students are asked to explore the characteristics of the materials and begin to make predictions as to their character and behavior. This is the discovery or exploration stage. In Stage 1, the skilled teacher may help students refine concepts to the point that when scientific terminology is encountered, students realize that they understood the concept even before it acquired a formal name. In Stage 2, more formal concepts are introduced. Students begin to understand how the world of science is described, and teachers determine how much talk versus discovery should be emphasized. In Stage 3, students apply the new concept in unfamiliar settings to deepen their understanding.

A more recent five-stage instructional model shares characteristics with the learning-cycle approach. This is how it is outlined in *Science for Life and Living*:

STEP 1: Engage the learner.

Activities are introduced that engage students with a problem or phenomenon. Such activities capture students' interest and enable them to make connections with what they know and can do.

STEP 2: Explore the concept.

Next, students participate in hands-on experiences through which they explore the concept further. They receive little explanation or terminology at this point because they are to define the problem or phenomenon in their own words. At this stage in the learning process, students are meant to acquire a common set of experiences so that they can help one another make sense of the concept. Students spend considerable time talking about their experiences, both to articulate their own understanding and to understand one another's point of view.

STEP 3: Explain the concept and define the terms.

Only after students have explored the concept independently are scientific explanations and terms for what they are studying introduced. Students then use the terms to describe what they have experienced and begin to examine how the explanation fits with what they already know.

STEP 4: Elaborate on the concept.

Students are given opportunities to apply the concept in new situations, or they are introduced to related ideas that they explore and explain using the information and experiences they have accumulated so far. Interaction between students is essential during the elaboration stage. By discussing their ideas with each other, students gain a deeper understanding of the concept.

In this stage, students continue to elaborate on their understanding and evaluate what they now know and what they have yet to figure out. Although the key word at this stage is evaluate, this does not indicate finality. Indeed, students will continue to construct their understanding of each broad concept throughout their lives.

The instructional approaches discussed earlier incorporate elements of this strategy. They might encompass introducing a new topic with two days of lecture and discussion, then students are given an open-ended question that requires application of the concepts presented in an experimental context.

The Teacher's Role in Inquiry-Based Instruction

In inquiry-based, student-driven investigations, teachers direct only a part of the action. In "real" science, there is no absolute authority to supply an answer that scientists can't find for themselves. No absolute authority can lend a hand by hinting to scientists that their investigation is on the right track or reassuring them at the conclusion of their efforts by confirming or rejecting the results. This very absence of an external source of authority motivates scientific inquiry and can make the attempt to solve a problem at once satisfying and frustrating, so the student's progress is enhanced if the teacher doesn't give students the answer or even tell them in detail how to get the answers. This is an intrinsic part of modeling the process of doing science.

Making a Mistake Isn't a Waste of Time

Not directing all the action isn't as easy as it may sound. Because teachers enter their profession with a desire to communicate knowledge, the temptation to supply an answer is sometimes very strong. As one teacher describes it, "For a teacher to stand there and let a student make really, really dumb mistakes and realize, if I just whispered two words into that student's ear, he or she could self-correct immediately—well, the temptation to whisper the two words becomes almost overpowering." There may also be pressure from other teachers and administrators who don't understand the significance of what looks like chaos in the classroom. Our teacher notes, "Your peers might say, 'What the hell's wrong with you? Your kids are still doing that same old lab? My kids have worked through four labs since you got started on that.'" Another says, "My kids are loud and they're having too much fun. Some people ask, 'How can they be learning physics?'"

The teacher who perseveres is the one who realizes that the "really, really dumb mistakes" students make in the course of doing science are not meaningless but intrinsic to the process of understanding science. The bodies of knowledge we call science were constructed in part because scientists made mistakes, were dissatisfied, and worked to discover the sources of their errors. One teacher first grasped the importance of this when a student, in the middle of a frustrating experiment, said to her, "Tell me if what I'm doing is right. I don't want to waste my time making a mistake." She recalls that the remark "turned me around as a science teacher. This lightbulb went on in my head and I thought, we've got to get kids to the point where they realize that making a mistake isn't a waste of time."

Teachers as Facilitators

What is the teacher's role? Teachers in inquiry-centered learning situations act as facilitators and resources. They create the environment in which investigations take place; they impart conceptual knowledge, mathematical and technical tools, and general guidelines at optimal moments. Teachers select learning experiences and adapt and design curricula to meet the interests, knowledge, abilities, and backgrounds of their students.

If science students have little experience with experimental approaches, the teacher may begin with a simple question, such as "What happens to the surface of a freshly cut potato?" expecting younger students or those with little background in science simply to observe that it turns brown. Older or more experienced students are challenged to devise ways of preventing the cut surface from turning brown. For the most advanced students, the challenge is to construct explanations for the change of color, explanations that must be tested through further experiments.

Advanced students bring to the problem their knowledge of chemistry (as well as biology) and their understanding of systems. Their analysis may emphasize that the potato surface is not an isolated object. Rather, it exists in an atmosphere that is normally air, but the potato could be placed in some other atmosphere or even immersed in a variety of liquids to investigate the browning process. Students' ability to generalize their knowledge can be assessed by asking them to investigate freshly cut apples instead of potatoes. Through such experiments, all students, regardless of their age or science background, will have grappled with some unifying concepts and processes in biology, chemistry and other sciences: systems, order, and organization; and evidence, models, and explanation.

While teams of students work, the teacher is quietly available, walking among the students, responding to calls for clarification, directing students to outside resources—the textbook, the library, computer data bases, perhaps even exchanging electronic mail with university faculty and researchers—or encouraging them to take full advantage of their classmates' knowledge. The teacher may help groups determine what mathematical or other conceptual tools are applicable to the problem, while refraining from giving them a specific strategy to follow, or the teacher may point out problems with the experimental design that need to be worked out.

Students work together as a community of learners; the teacher ensures that they listen to each other with respect, reflect and build on one another's ideas, demand evidence to support opinions, assist each other in drawing conclusions, and challenge the facts, assumptions, and arguments underlying different points of view (Jones and Fennimore 1990, 17). After the investigations are completed, the teacher moderates the discussion as groups of students share and critique each other's findings. The teacher helps students make connections between their experiments and their knowledge of scientific concepts; encourages students to reflect on the meaning of their work; and reads and comments on their lab reports, suggesting improvements when appropriate. That this is possibility, not pie-in-the-sky, is amply demonstrated by examples of teacher instructional approaches given earlier.

Because students are initiating much of the action, and any given day's events may be unpredictable, teachers must surrender some degree of control over class activities. Because close attention is given to the quality and depth of students' learning, assessing student progress can be time-consuming and difficult. Both the teacher and the students participate in the ongoing assessment of student performance. But for a task such as reviewing group lab portfolios, one teacher reports, "I'll sit in front of a fireplace for a hundred hours. I'll write whole paragraphs of commentary sometimes. If you're expecting quality work from the students, then you have to evaluate their work in a quality fashion."

The satisfaction for teachers who choose to be facilitators comes in seeing their students develop as independent learners. This is satisfying to the students, as well. "Learning how to stand up in front of a crowd and defend what you believe in because you've done an experiment with sufficient accuracy that not even the teacher can move you away from—that finding is in fact very, very satisfying," is how one classroom veteran describes his students' experiences.

How Much Structure—How Much Freedom?

How much freedom to explore should be given to students? How much control should they have in initiating their inquiries? Few teachers attempt to offer labs that are entirely open-ended, in which students come up with questions on any topic that interests them, design an experimental protocol entirely on their own, find or build whatever equipment they need, take as much time as they need, and decide when the investigation is finished. Regardless of how much freedom is allowed, teachers must provide as much guidance as necessary to ensure that all students acquire the expected knowledge, skills, and understanding.

Some teachers such as Carlyon, present their students with a specific situation—thermometers wrapped in socks of different fabric—as well as a specific question—what temperatures will the thermometers read? Mestre and Lochhead (1990) describe an approach called "structured inquiry." The teacher offers a specific topic but no specific questions. Instead, through discussion, students generate a number of hypotheses and procedures that are explored separately by teams, with the results shared upon completion of the projects. This resembles the approach of Skinner, who gives her students a specific topic, slime mold, and asks them to generate a question about the topic within fixed parameters. (For example, be able to answer the question in a given number of days.) Other teachers, like Winemiller, present a situation, bottle rockets, that yields a number of possible questions. Through discussion, groups of students select a particular question to address, and the different groups work in parallel.

Among the principal reasons for maintaining some structure in the classroom is ensuring that the significant scientific concepts are introduced. Those concepts are clearly delineated in the NSES and AAAS standards documents. Winemiller knows that the bottle rocket experiment will lead to a discussion of Newtonian mechanics; Carlyon designed the thermometer experiment to teach concepts of heat and temperature; and Skinner introduces her students to the inquiry mode and experimental design with the slime mold project. In deciding how much and in what way to structure investigations, teachers are making decisions about the concepts to be introduced to students and the scientific procedures that students will employ. At the same time, teachers know they must surrender some control over classroom activities. "You have to be a risk taker," says Winemiller. "How do we know exactly what we're going to encounter? In fact, I do know we cover a great deal. If I didn't know that I wouldn't teach this way."

These teachers also know that they may not cover as many topics as some of their colleagues. But they are committed to "less is more"—to ensuring that their students thoroughly know, understand, and are able to do that science to which they are introduced. For example, Skinner may focus on only two or three organ systems so that her biology students develop a strong model of what a system is. The students are encouraged to link the model to broader biological concepts such as the organization of life and the relation of structure to function. "If they have that experience," she says, "then should they learn about a new system, they have a conceptual framework within which to put the additional facts."

Teaching Resources: Introducing the New and Transforming the Familiar

An emphasis on inquiry-based instruction requires a fresh understanding of such familiar instructional materials as textbooks, written problem sets, and reference books. Instead of regularly basing assignments on such materials, in the inquiry-based classroom, these materials serve the students as resources to be drawn on as needed in their investigations.

Here's an example drawn from Earth and Space Science, Content Standard D: As a result of their activities in grades 9–12, all students should develop an understanding of energy in the earth system; geochemical cycles; origin and evolution of the earth system; and origin and evolution of the universe (NSES 1996, 187). These are very broad themes and can be addressed in many ways. One area of study is the water cycle, which students view as a carrier of material; however, as they deepen their understanding, they will recognize that it is an important agent for energy transfer. The water cycle provides students with opportunities to work with information from their immediate surroundings.

Aspects of the water cycle can be studied in all regions of

the country with information obtained from weather bureaus. Exercises can be devised that require students to access local data, collect some of their own, and finally account for the water cycle's influence on their own environment. As the standards suggest, "It is important to maintain the spirit of inquiry by focusing the teaching on questions that can be answered by using observational data, the knowledge base of science, and the processes of learning" (NSES 1996, 189). Work in grades 9–12 must build on the knowledge, understanding, and ability to do science that students have acquired in their earlier grades.

Technology can be an important resource in inquiry-based instruction, as long as students do not rely too heavily on it. Winemiller's students prepare their lab reports on computers, using word processing, graphing, and spreadsheet software. But they also learn to solve equations without spreadsheets and to employ such low-tech devices as homemade astrolabes and milk crates as rocket cages. "It's easy to lose touch with what's going on when a computer does all the work for you," says the *Water Rockets I–III Teacher Handbook*, developed by Winemiller and Bonnstetter (1994, 14). On the other hand, using computers can help students save time and energy for more challenging and interesting and perhaps totally new aspects of their investigations. With the advent of battery-operated computer-based laboratory recording devices, which can record data in the field, students can monitor the physical conditions of biological systems within their local communities or their own acceleration as they ride amusement park roller coasters. Students can even gather raw data useful to their community by monitoring habitats near the school that have not been studied by others.

Developing resources for student investigations is not an easy task. Many teachers gather materials via creative collaboration with colleagues. Winemiller was first introduced to bottle rockets as a teaching tool when he studied science education with Ron Bonnstetter. Over the years, and with Bonnstetter's continuing support, Winemiller developed the bottle rocket experiment into a richer and more versatile experience than the one that was originally presented to him.

As students are allowed increasing freedom to pose and answer their own questions, it is more likely that teachers will be asked for help they cannot immediately provide, because what students need may fall outside the scope of teachers' expertise or subject-matter speciality. When the teacher and students perceive themselves as members of a common learning community, they can collaboratively seek the answers. If the answer is provided by students and is new to the teacher, so much the better. Further, classrooms may have access to Internet and World Wide Web sites which provide information that is not available from local resources.

Assessment in the Inquiry-Based Classroom

The goal for the nation is that "all students should achieve scientific literacy." While assessments will be made at various levels, our concern here is the classroom, where teachers are responsible for assessment. Regardless of the particular assessment approach being used, teachers must ensure that evaluations of student performance are firmly aligned with the learning goals outlined in national, state, and district documents and with ongoing classroom instruction.

Assessment must be viewed in a broad context. The following statement appears in the Association for Supervision and Curriculum Development's "Clarifying Terms" section of *A Practical Guide to Alternative Assessment*: "The fundamental role of assessment is to provide authentic and meaningful feedback for improving student learning, instructional practice, and educational options" (Herman, Ashbacher, and Winters 1992, vi).

Assessment of student performance in an inquiry-based classroom involves asking students to:

- generate rather than choose a response;
- actively accomplish complex and significant tasks; and
- solve realistic or authentic problems.

Such achievement in classrooms is assessed through:

- exhibitions
- investigations
- demonstrations
- written or oral responses
- journals
- portfolios.

Elements of this approach to assessment can easily be identified in the efforts of Winemiller, Carlyon, and Skinner. "Making observations of student performance during instructional activities" is an ongoing responsibility of the teacher (NSES, Assessment Standard D 1996, 84). Assessment is not a separate activity.

As noted in Chapter 3, in the inquiry-based classroom, assessment and learning are viewed as two sides of the same coin. In fact, "authentic assessment," a term that is widely used in the wake of recent education reforms, reflects this synergy. The national standards define an assessment as authentic "when students are engaged in assessment tasks that are similar in form to tasks in which they will engage in their lives outside the classroom or are similar to the activities of scientists" (NSES, Assessment Standard D, 83).

The laboratory report, when its format encourages students to organize, structure, and process their thinking, is one important indicator of student progress toward knowing, understanding, and being able to do science. This progress cannot be assessed solely by customary techniques such as multiple-choice and short-answer questions. Teachers are challenging students to grow as thinkers, and their thinking should be multilayered, complex, and embedded in context.

Laboratory reports, such as the samples given on pages 46–48, can give students the opportunity to demonstrate not only their methodological skills but also the thinking that led to a particular experimental design and the formulation of their conclusions. Students may be asked to explain in their laboratory reports how they would do their experiment differently; what inferences they can draw from the reports of other students

Laboratory reports such as these give students the opportunity to show the thinking that led to certain conclusions.

Sept. 6th

Can you categorize these?

1
- The freshly cut piece is still wet, crisp and smells almost acidic.
- The skin is on and it is flexable
- The inside is very white & translucent

2
- The next one is very soft all the way through.
- There isn't as much water and the skin is almost falling off
- It smells like a baked potato and it crumbles when you try to bend it
- The inside is much more yellow

3
- The inside is light brown, not uniform.
- when you scrape the brown off the inside is wet and crisp like the fresh one
- The skin is still on and it is flexable
- It smells like the fresh one and is translucid w/ out the brown layer.

QUESTIONS:

- what kind of chemical / substance / equipment could block whatever is turning it brown

- could you take something thick like nail polish and write your name to block EVERYTHING –

- Lemon juice, acidic, keeps apples from turning brown – (good!)

- How long does it have to be exposed in order to turn brown. Will I see do it?

variables

light vs Dark
acid on it
something to block it   great ideas
submerge in water
the cooking / heat source

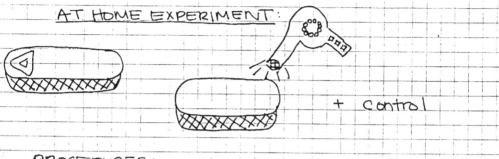

AT HOME EXPERIMENT:

+ control

PROCEDURES:

- On one I painted a triangle of clear nail polish, hopping to block the brown stuff from comming similar to the oil, but a thicker substance

- A hairdryer was propped 8 inches above the potato while another was set aside to calculate the speed of the browning & see weather heat was a factor

- After 25 min. of heat, I removed the hair dryer and let both sit overnight.

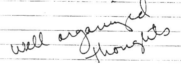

well organized thoughts

OBSERVATIONS:

- The 1st potato browned while the nail polished triangle remained white - this was ≈ 30 min. later
- The control browned after 25 min. and the one under heat turned dry at the top and got a thin layer of white crust around the edge. (most likely dry potato)
- It was slightly yellow and smelled like baked potato
- After sitting overnight the heated potato turned black and slimey.

→ ● Do we know what this is?

Potato Lab

piece 1 - has been cooked
is softer, like a baked potato
yellow ___ or inside shrunk
the skin has pulled away from the inside
cracked
dry
smells different than the ones that have not cooked

piece 2 - brown - mostly around the edges
dry ≠ (drier (than the others))
brown so far is only on the surface

piece 3 - thinly sliced
just cut
wet
~~transparent~~ translucent in places
~~at~~ white, but after 5 min it started to turn brown

- why does the potato turn brown?
- does it have to do with oxygen?
- does it have to do with sugar?
- does it have to do with pH?   great
- what effect does cooking have on ideas
- does it have to do with light?
- does it have to do with water?

| oxygen |
| light |
| sugar |
| water |
| pH |
| metal |
| carbon dioxide |
| salt |
| pressure |

Enzymos
temp
juice   ammonia
change pH - Acids Bases
cook it
freeze it

disprove
light
metal

Acid / Base

$2N H_2SO_4$ / Sodium Hydroxide

I put 1 thin slice of potato in 3 ~~three~~ dishes Can this be organized better?

in dish one - Base] looks ~~dark green~~ yellow (1:37) / no change (1:56)

~~dish~~

dish two - Acid] no change in color (1:37) / no change (1:56)

dish three - nothing] turned brown quickly (1:37) / no change (1:56)

temp

I froze one slice of potato and at the same time left one out at room temp. 2 hours later the one in the freezer was the same color, but the one at room temp was brown. I set them out in room temp. to let the frozen one thaw. 25 min. later it started turning ~~brown~~ orange around the edges. Does freezing permanently change the potato?

light

2

I put one slice of potato in the dark uncovered and at the same time I put another slice in a lighted room uncovered. 20 min. later they both turned brown equally and groups; what criticisms or questions are raised by other students' reports; and what follow-up experiments might be conducted to test new hypotheses. By responding to such questions, students not only demonstrate what they know and can do, but are also encouraged to evaluate their own work and reflect on its significance. In this way, as Wolf and Pistone put it in *Taking Full Measure*, assessment becomes "not so much a test as an episode of learning" (1991, 9).

In Winemiller's class, portfolios containing group laboratory reports are an important element in assessment. Students are given opportunities throughout the year to develop and improve their portfolios in response to his critiques. Winemiller believes this emphasis on improvement and ongoing assessment, rather than on assessment at the close of a unit of study or a course, is part of modeling real science. In the world of real science and engineering, progress is characterized by ups and downs, but over time the depth and extent of knowledge increase.

With so much focus on teamwork and group activities, especially in experimental settings, how does the teacher distinguish individual progress from group progress? One solution is to emphasize multidimensional assessment. The maplecopter experiment described earlier offers an example of such an assessment. A summary group report provides the basis for assessing the quality of each group's experimental efforts. Individual progress is evaluated via two examinations written in class without the benefit of interaction with other students— one based on individual observations of maple seeds prior to the start of the group investigation, the other responding to questions after all groups have made their presentations. In addition, students are asked to assess the quality of their own collaboration within a group, and both students and teachers evaluate the quality of the presentations.

This multidimensional assessment generates a great deal of paper that the teacher must painstakingly evaluate. But it means that individual progress as well as collective achievement is fully evaluated. Winemiller assesses individual contributions to a group project by asking students to complete a form on which they evaluate their own contribution and that of other group members. Winemiller tells his students that "If four or five of the students in your group evaluate you as having done only 5 percent of the work, then I use that as a factor in calculating your grade."

All of the teachers who provided material for this book give tests of some kind, though the tests are often linked to students' experimental efforts. Carlyon's final exam includes this question: "Take the generator you made two-and-a-half months ago and explain, based on your knowledge today, how you could improve the performance of that generator." Carlyon considers this an excellent vehicle for assessing individual understanding: "You either know what you're talking about or you don't know. You can't fake it." The test also serves as a culminating episode of learning, one that requires students to make connections among different course experiences and once again to assume the role of a scientist.

The goal of scientific literacy for all students requires assessment that is fair to all. Howard Gardner (Gardner 1983) postulates the existence of possibly five different intelligences: linguistic, musical, logical-mathematical, spatial, and bodily-kinesthetic. Herman et al. (1992) elaborate, pointing out that each individual has strength in at least two or three of these areas and that there is great variation in the modes and speeds with which people acquire knowledge, in the attention and memory capabilities they can apply to knowledge acquisition and performance, and in the ways in which they can demonstrate the personal meaning they have created. Thus, to succeed with all students, instruction and assessment must tap more than one type of intelligence and teachers must be committed to the proposition that all students can learn (Herman et al. 1992, 16).

Some students enrolled in science courses may be strong in areas of intelligence other than the logical-mathematical, but they can still have a successful encounter with science and learn to think scientifically. Assessment in the science classroom should be broad enough to involve a student's multiple intelligences, so that each student can experience success in the study of science. Skilled use of language, artistic ways of illustrating laboratory reports, the capacity to describe movement as in dance can all contribute to the experience of doing science. Teachers need to find ways to reward students for their capacity to experience, contribute to, and demonstrate scientific understanding.

An inquiry-based curriculum does not isolate skills and facts. Rather, it emphasizes both through meaningful, complex tasks embedded in increasingly challenging environments. Materials and content are structured so that students gradually regulate their own learning. This approach ensures that learning motivates students and encourages them in terms of both competence and confidence. Self-assessment of progress by both individual students and groups is a very powerful result of an inquiry-based approach to learning science.

The National Science Education Standards speak of two aspects of assessment—student achievement and the opportunity to learn. The classroom teacher assesses student achievement—a focus of our attention in this book. But national assessment standards are equally applicable to assessing teachers, schools, and school districts. These participants in the learning community need to help ensure that students are provided with ample opportunities to learn.

National Consensus on Science Goals

Teachers who commit themselves to inquiry-based instruction must be risk takers. The hard work and long hours, the surrender of some control in the classroom, the anxiety of replacing familiar, tested instructional methods with unfamiliar ones are burdens that teachers adopting this approach willingly assume in the interests of their students. But the burdens should not be heavier than necessary. Schools, education systems, and governments can do a great deal to make it easier for teachers to make substantive commitments that will benefit their students.

With respect to content, both the NSES and Benchmarks documents emphasize the "less is more" approach and identify core scientific concepts that are found in all disciplines. NSES elaborates eight categories of content standards as well as identifying a relatively small number of science concepts to be understood and applied deeply. The first category is "unifying concepts and processes in science." This content standard is developed for grades K–12, based on recognition that an understanding of conceptual frameworks and experimental procedures needs to be introduced as early as possible in a student's education and emphasized throughout the school experience. The seven additional NSES categories of content standards are science as inquiry, physical science, life science, earth and space science, science and technology, science in personal and social perspectives, and the history and nature of science. These seven categories are elaborated separately for grades K–4, 5–8, and 9–12, emphasizing increasing complexity at higher grade levels. When all students experience success in each of these categories at K–4 and 5–8 levels, the opportunities for science teachers in grades 9–12 to ensure science literacy for all will be greatly enhanced.

The NSES Program Standards provide criteria for judging the quality of and identify the necessary conditions for school science programs. These standards recommend consistency with all components of national standards within and across grade levels; a program of science study based on inquiry that is developmentally appropriate, interesting, and relevant to students' lives; coordination of science programs with mathematics programs; and ensuring student access to appropriate and sufficient resources, including quality teachers, time, materials and equipment, adequate and safe work space, and access to the community.

The Program Standards also address the importance of providing opportunities for *all* students to achieve the national standards. The NSES document supports teachers in recommending that the entire community share responsibility for science education. ■

Epilogue

Scientists do carry on a conversation, but not with nature. The conversation scientists carry on is with each other.

(Bruffee 1992)

Exploring the World of Science: Global Warming

Rice University Professor Ronald Sass describes his experiences with a high school junior named Hai, who was encouraged by a former teacher, Peggy Campbell, to pursue his personal interest in the subject of global warming. Hai's independent research became the basis for a successful science fair project. More important, it gave him a rich, authentic experience of what scientists do.

Hai had a keen interest in global change. He had learned that human activity was causing the concentration of certain atmospheric trace gases to increase and that this would eventually cause serious global climate changes. But he had many unanswered questions. He didn't notice any change in the air he breathed or any detectable change in the climate. What could he do to demonstrate to himself that a problem, or even a potential problem, really existed?

Hai couldn't answer these questions in his high school science course because the study of global warming itself is relatively new and the experiments necessary to observe such global effects are usually too expensive and too lengthy for a high school science lab course. At Rice University, however, Sass and his colleagues study the natural and anthropogenic processes that produce atmospheric methane and other trace gases.

Hai talked to Sass and, as a consequence, began haunting

the Rice lab after school and during vacations. Hai also started experimenting on his own. He knew that several animals produce methane, particularly cows and other ruminants. He discovered that methane is also produced by resident bacteria in the guts of termites, and that the lowly termite is considered by some to be a significant source of atmospheric methane.

Hai asked Sass and his colleagues whether insects other than termites were known methane producers. They said that was very probable, but few data were available on the subject. Hai decided that, using the Rice laboratory facilities, he would carry out his own investigation of insects as methane producers. His experimental plan was straightforward. He would collect several different insects and place one or more of the same species in a container equipped with an intake tube for introducing air and an outlet tube to collect the air plus any methane produced. The container would be filled with ambient air and sealed for a short time, then a sample would be taken for analysis and the system would be flushed with air for the next measurement period.

Hai decided to work with six species of insects and feed four different diets to each. His matrix of variables resulted in 6 x 4 or 24 different experimental setups. To measure methane production, Hai figured that he would need to collect data at different times of the day. He decided to try every 3 hours during one 24-hour period or 8 samples per experiment. His simple experimental design suddenly required making 192 measurements!

The following week when Hai returned, he analyzed his samples and found they all contained levels of methane significantly above the normal atmospheric amounts. Hai was ready to believe that he was really on to something. However, every sample showed approximately the same high methane level, indicating that all the insects, regardless of diet, produced nearly the same amount of methane, a rather unlikely result. Sass asked Hai, "What level of methane did you find in your empty control chamber?" Looking again at the output from the gas chromatograph, he found that the control results were also abnormally high.

Hai wondered, "What should I do?" He answered his own question: "Find the experimental problem." "Correct, but how?" Sass asked. "Where did you fill the chambers?" "In my living room at home," said Hai. So he got several gas syringes and began sampling the air in different homes and yards. Hai discovered that his results were invalid because the methane level in his house was three times higher than in the outside air. It was later concluded that the 50-year-old house had a gas leak.

Hai then refilled his containers after taking samples in his front yard where he found a normal methane level in the air. He fed his subjects different diets (fructose, sucrose, starch, and cellulose). This time Hai got the results he expected. Some of the insects did indeed produce methane, and furthermore, there seemed to be an effect due to diet. The final results were quite surprising. Cockroaches and bessbugs were the significant methane producers. The rest of the insects produced negligible amounts of methane.

What did Hai learn from his investigation? To ask a meaningful question in science, one must first find out what is known about a subject, what questions remain unanswered, and what methods are available to answer them. He learned to formulate his own questions. He learned how to design an experiment, recognize false data, and adjust his procedures to obtain meaningful data. Hai learned the excitement of discovery and the disappointment of temporary failure. He learned that science is hard work, frustrating, perplexing, time-consuming, and often presents as many questions as it answers. He also learned that science is exciting, leads to a greater understanding of the natural world, and is not so difficult that it cannot be mastered.

Hai received a number of awards for his efforts, including a prize for science writing. The latter was particularly rewarding because Hai had first become friends with Peggy Campbell, the teacher who started him on this quest, when he was a seventh-grade science student in her special education class, placed there because, as a recent immigrant, he knew no English.

Lifelong Learning and Professional Development

The ultimate goal is the scientifically literate person, and science teachers are responsible for starting all students along that path. Scientific literacy should continue to develop and grow within all students throughout their lives. The scientifically literate person is defined in *Science for All Americans* as someone who:

1. has integrated knowledge of science, mathematics, and technology;

2. has a deep understanding of scientific concepts and processes; and

3. appreciates that both the learning and the practice of science are dynamic and constructed.

For science teachers charged with setting students on this learning pathway, professional development must also be a continuous, lifelong process. The teacher we're talking about:

1. has integrated knowledge of science, mathematics, and technology;

2. has a deep conceptual understanding of how learning can be optimized for students with different learning styles; and

3. appreciates that both the learning and the practice of science are dynamic and constructed.

"The development of pedagogical content knowledge by teachers mirrors what we know about learning by students; it can be fully developed only through continuous experience. But experience is not sufficient. Teachers must have opportunities to engage in analysis of the individual components of pedagogical content knowledge—science learning, learning, and pedagogy—and make connections between them." This statement is part of an extended discussion contained in the NSES Standards for Professional Development of Teachers.

Such pedagogical content knowledge is demonstrated by our colleagues Jake Winemiller, Peggy O'Neill Skinner, Earl Carlyon, and Ronald Sass in the manner in which they conduct their classes, emphasizing high levels of content-centered individual and group activity, and by the manner in which they assess the learning that transpires in the classroom. They have willingly shared their insights with us; we have become part of their professional community of learners. We must now activitate within our own spheres of influence a community dedicated to supporting and realizing science standards in the classroom. And, in addition, to encourage students to become like Hai, interested in pursuing questions even outside the classroom and, we hope, to become lifelong learners in science. ■

Editor's Note

It is our hope that this book will assist teachers and teacher educators to bring science standards to life for all students by implementing the best approaches currently in practice in high schools. Actively engaging students in the process of inquiry and exploration, with a belief that everyone can learn in such a setting, increases each and every student's chance to succeed in acquiring scientific knowledge. Questioning, thinking, guessing, speculating, and exchanging ideas and information all foster a teaching and learning environment for teacher and student alike. If we can offer this opportunity to every student and help teachers open up the classroom to the practices and excitement of science, we will surely go a long way toward increasing scientific literacy in and out of the school setting. It is, after all, lifelong learning that best serves every individual and the overall society in a changing, competitive world. We believe the skills acquired in learning science can be part of a whole learning experience, making connections across the disciplines easier to identify. This book is intended as a first step in working toward that goal.

**The National Center for
Cross-Disciplinary Teaching and Learning**

BIBLIOGRAPHY

Baron, J., Principal Investigator. 1993. "Exploring the MapleCopter." In *Connecticut Common Core of Learning Assessment.* Connecticut State Department of Education and the National Science Foundation.

Benchmarks for Science Literacy. 1995. Washington, DC: American Association for the Advancement of Science, Project 2061.

Bridgman, Percy. 1960. *The Reflections of a Physicist.* New York: Philosophical Library.

Brooks, J.G. and M.G. Brooks.1993. *In Search of Understanding: The Case for Constructivist Classrooms.* Alexandria, VA: Association for Supervision and Curriculum Development.

Bruffee, K.A. 1992. "Science in a Postmodern World," *Change*, September/October: 18–25.

Gardner, Howard. 1983. *Frames of Mind: The Theory of Multiple Intelligences.* New York: Basic Books.

Gleick, James. 1992. *Genius: The Life and Science of Richard Feynman.* New York: Vintage.

Greeno, James G. 1992. "Mathematical and Scientific Thinking in Classrooms and Other Situations." In *Enhancing Thinking Skills in the Sciences and Mathematics.* Diane F. Halpern, ed. Hillsdale, NJ: Lawrence Erlbaum.

Herman, Joan L., P.R. Ashbacher, and Lynn Winters. 1992. *A Practical Guide to Alternative Assessment.* Alexandria, VA: Association for Supervision and Curriculum Development.

Mestre, J.P. and J. Lochhead. 1990. *Academic Preparation in Science.* New York: College Entrance Examination Board.

National Science Education Standards. 1996. National Committee on Science Education Standards and Assessment, National Research Council.

Resnick, Lauren B. 1987. *Education and Learning to Think.* Washington, DC: National Academy Press.

Resnick, Lauren B. and L.E. Klopfer, ed. 1989. *Toward the Thinking Curriculum: Current Cognitive Research.* Alexandria, VA: ASCD.

Resources for Science Literacy: Professional Development. 1996. New York: Oxford University Press.

Rutherford, F.J. and A. Ahlgren. 1990. *Science for All Americans.* New York: Oxford University Press.

Winemiller, J. and R. Bonnstetter. 1994. *Water Rockets I-III. Video Program and Teacher Handbook.* Encinitas, CA: Insights Visual Production.

Wolf, Dennie and Nancy Pistone. 1991. *Taking Full Measure: Rethinking Assessment through the Arts.* New York: College Entrance Examination Board.